M000073628

To:

_____

From:

_____

Date:

_____

Miracle Moments of Faith

© 2010 Christian Art Gifts, RSA
      Christian Art Gifts Inc., IL, USA

Designed by Christian Art Gifts

Images used under license from Shutterstock.com

Scripture quotations are taken from *The Message*. Copyright © by Eugene H. Peterson, 1993, 1994, 1995, 1996, 2000, 2001, 2002. Used by permission of NavPress Publishing Group.

Scripture quotations are taken from the *Holy Bible,* New Century Version®. Copyright © 2005 by Thomas Nelson, Inc. Used by permission. All rights reserved.

Scripture quotations are taken from the Holy Bible, New International Version® NIV®. Copyright © 1973, 1978, 1984 by International Bible Society. Used by permission of Zondervan Publishing House. All rights reserved.

Printed in China

ISBN 978-1-77036-437-0

10 11 12 13 14 15 16 17 18 19 – 10 9 8 7 6 5 4 3 2 1

MIRACLE
MOMENTS
of FAITH

KAREN MOORE

christian
art gifts.

Contents

For all who live by the gift of faith and open the door to miracles. Blessing upon blessing to you.

~ Karen

Introduction

Miracle Moments are noteworthy because we don't expect them. We might even assume them to be out of the ordinary, a thing of the past that only happened to people in the Bible.

Yet, as we look at the collected works of the Gospels and the Old Testament, it seems clear that everyday miracles were part of an ordinary believer's life.

Maybe then, the advent of miracles happening in our own lives has more to do with our belief system than with God's willingness to work in that special way.

Let the pages of this book remind you of miracles that happened to our biblical ancestors and help you see why they are still relevant today. We'll look at miraculous answers to prayer and strengthen our faith and resolve to be continual prayer warriors.

We'll read amazing stories of healing miracles, miracles of God's provision, and finally, we'll look at those tender miracles of grace that happen all the time in the lives of people everywhere.

As you read about these Miracle Moments, may your heart be opened to those that God has waiting for you. May you see Him in fresh ways as He helps you discover more of His presence in your life and in your hopes and dreams.

May you be blessed, dear reader, with a lifetime of love and precious Miracle Moments all of your own.

Through the miracle of His love,

Karen Moore

7

Section One
Miracle Moments of Healing

Hezekiah Battles a Bully

One miraculous Old Testament story comes from Isaiah and centers around the king of Judah, Hezekiah. Let's look at the miracles God created in the life of this king and see if we can relate them to our current history.

Here are some bits and pieces from the Bible narrative. We'll start where the king of Assyria is basically trying to bully Hezekiah into NOT believing in the one true God.

"The great king, the king of Assyria, says: What can you trust in now? You say you have battle plans and power for war, but your words mean nothing. Whom are you trusting for help so that you turn against me? Look, you are depending on Egypt to help you, but Egypt is like a splintered walking stick.

If you lean on it for help, it will stab your hand and hurt you. The king of Egypt will hurt all those who depend on him. You might say, 'We are depending on the LORD our God,' but Hezekiah destroyed the LORD's altars and the places of worship. Hezekiah told Judah and Jerusalem, 'You must worship only at this one altar.'"

ISAIAH 36:4-7 NCV

Further on, the king of Assyria continues. "Don't let Hezekiah fool you, saying 'The LORD will save us.' Has a god of any other nation saved his people from the power of the king of Assyria?" (Isaiah 36:18 NCV)

Hezekiah didn't back down though and he didn't let the bullying get to him; he didn't react in fear. Being wise in the ways of the Creator, he went directly to the temple of the Lord, sought out the prophet Isaiah and started praying.

This is where things begin to get very interesting.

God's Answer to Bullies

Isaiah offers some great advice from the Lord. He tells Hezekiah's officers that they have no reason to fear the king of Assyria. The Lord already has a plan in place to answer the boastful king and protect His people. Even though the Assyrian king kept taunting him, telling Hezekiah to stop believing that his God would save him, Hezekiah continued to do the right thing. He kept on praying.

And What About You?

If you've ever put your heart and soul, everything you have, at the Lord's feet and tried in every way possible to communicate with Him, you probably understand what Hezekiah did as he pleaded for God's direction and mercy concerning the threats of the king.

The part for us to bear in mind is that Hezekiah didn't give in. **He kept waiting for the Lord's direction.** Finally the Lord answered Hezekiah and His response was chilling.

Isaiah 37

Isaiah reported the Lord's response as follows, "This is what the LORD, the God of Israel, says: 'You prayed to Me about Sennacherib king of Assyria. So this is what the LORD has said against Sennacherib:

"You have insulted Me and spoken against Me. You have a proud look on your face, which is against Me, the Holy One of Israel!"

"Because you rage against Me, and because I have heard your proud words, I will put My hook in your nose and My bit in your mouth. Then I will force you to leave My country the same way you came.

"The strong love of the LORD All-Powerful will make this happen. Then the angel of the LORD went out and killed one hundred eighty-five thousand men in the Assyrian camp" (vv. 21-23, 29, 32-36 NCV).

As a further note, the Bible reports that Sennacherib was later killed by his own sons.

How Can We Relate to This?

First of all, it appears that Hezekiah, although a godly man, made unfortunate choices concerning where and when people could worship God. He set down rules that were publicly known and ones for which the king of Assyria could ridicule him.

How many of us have made decisions that, if made public, might bring some hoots and hollers from those who like to give faith a bad name? One of the devices of the world is to try to prove to us that God doesn't really exist or that our thinking about Him is somehow faulty.

Hezekiah left himself open to rebuke, and we do that sometimes as well. We cannot underestimate the conse-quences of our choices – as Hezekiah learned the hard way.

How Bullies Work

If you've ever faced a bully, you might have a better perspective on the exchange between these two kings.

Isn't it the nature of a bully to try to hit you when you're down, to find your Achilles heel and make you as fearful and uncomfortable as possible?

Isn't it also the nature of a bully to try to get the support of those around you so that you feel even more ashamed and ridiculed in front of your peers?

The bully wants you to feel weakened; he wants you to believe that you are defeated.

But what he doesn't know is that ...

"When you are weak, God's POWER is made perfect in you."

2 Corinthians 12:9 NCV

So What Do You Do
When Faced with a Bully?

If wisdom prevails, you take the assault and bring it before the Lord to see if He is willing to enter the challenge with you.

Insulting the Creator God may have seemed unimportant to Sennacherib, but we're reminded that God hears everything and is very aware of the battles we face.

He sees our hearts and knows the motivations of every one of His children.

If we truly understand that, we can trust that He is indeed invested in the outcome and will take a stand to set things right.

Waiting for God's Answer

After Hezekiah poured out his heart and his concerns before God, he waited for God's answer. We don't know how long he waited but it appears that God's answer was fairly quick and to the point.

God reminded Sennacherib that He, God, was the One who created all those aspects of life that made the king believe he was somehow powerful.

God even said, "King of Assyria, surely you have heard. Long ago, I, the LORD, planned these things. Long ago I designed them, and now I have made them happen. I allowed you to turn those strong, walled cities into piles of rocks" (ISAIAH 37:26).

God Is the Author of Our Good

Sometimes we lose sight of who is really behind any success we might think we have. If we become short-sighted, we might even believe that we are responsible for the good that happens to us.

In truth, only God is the author of our good, and He set the course of it long before we arrived on the scene. Sennacherib lost sight of this truth, if he had ever known it.

God's Hook

Finally, God says something unsettling to Sennacherib. He says, "I know when you rest, when you come and go, and how you rage against Me. Because you rage against Me, and because I have heard your proud words, I will put My hook in your nose and My bit in your mouth" (Isaiah 37:28-29 NCV).

This clear declaration from God says the tide is about to turn, because He's ready to fight. When you catch a fish, it usually ends up with a hook in its mouth and, after some squirming, doesn't get away. It ends up being dinner. If you put a bit in the mouth of a horse, it goes the direction you want it to go, obeying your commands.

It appears God was suggesting death, or at least total obedience, and that the king of Assyria was going to have trouble eating his words.

Getting the Hook

In our own lives, we might see that sometimes God has had to deal with us in similar ways. He might not have hooked us like a fish or demanded total obedience from us outside of His gift of free will, but maybe He allowed us to be hooked on something that wasn't good for us, something that was actually deadening to our spirits.

Maybe we spent time addicted to something that really hurt us, like smoking, alcohol, or gambling. Our addictions changed the course of our lives and we were not able to hear God's voice.

We could not even correct our course without His help, yet we probably believed we were in charge of our lives. We have probably all behaved like Sennacherib did in one way or another.

God's Redeeming Miracle

The miracle, though, is that God doesn't leave us in the lurch. He finds a way to step in and turn the evil into good. He finds a way to redeem us yet again when our hearts are open to His leading.

His angel may not have to come and slay our demons, but He has to guard and guide us, and that requires from us to surrender to Him.

Hezekiah surrendered his life and will to God and that's why He was able to hear the response to his prayers and believe them. The king of Assyria, on the other hand, was a "self-made" man. If he had been a "God-made" man, his life would have yielded a different result. Let's thank God for granting us Miracle Moments of faith.

Moving on, we see God's love and faithfulness provided other miracles in the life of Hezekiah. One was receiving healing from a near-death experience.

Hezekiah's Healing

An old proverb says, "Unless we change direction, we are likely to end up where we are going."

In this biblical account, Hezekiah was dying. God even told him he would die. That must have seemed pretty definite, yet Hezekiah didn't give up. He turned his head to the wall and asked God to change the direction.

Isaiah 38 tells us this, "Hezekiah turned toward the wall and prayed to the LORD, 'LORD, please remember that I have always obeyed You. I have given myself completely to You and have done what You said was right.' Then Hezekiah cried loudly".

Speaking through Isaiah, God answered the king, "I have heard your prayer and seen your tears. So I will add fifteen years to your life. I will save you and this city from the king of Assyria; I will defend this city" (vv. 2-3, 5-6 NCV).

God's Purpose

One thing seems certain: Whether we look at the life of an ancient king who received an extra fifteen years of life by God's grace and mercy, or we look at the lives of those around us and see people who have escaped death through what we call miraculous circumstances, we must conclude that the reason is that God has a purpose that must still be worked out for that person.

Sometimes we might know what the purpose is, other times only God knows.

Hezekiah's Tears and His Miracle Moment of Faith

Hezekiah cried real tears when he asked God to grant him more time. We may understand those tears if we've ever been in a position to plead for more time ourselves.

We want more time to live, to become, to give back to God those things we know we've missed along the way.

Perhaps we would each experience a Miracle Moment of faith if we simply looked at each day as a gift and gave God praise.

Look at each day as a gift and give God praise.

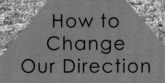

How to Change Our Direction

Imagine if we could see each day as a miracle given to us so that we can learn, observe, praise, honor, and give back something that God has waited patiently for us to recognize? Hezekiah got fifteen extra years. We don't know whether we are living on extra years or simply the ones already written in the Book of Life for us, but we must live them as though we are eternally grateful for every moment.

That would indeed be a miracle to help us change our direction.

Current Healing Miracles

A young man in Costa Rica shared a story with me about his family. He is married and has three sons, two of which are twins. When his twin sons were just seven months old, one of them was diagnosed with a tumor on his kidney that threatened to take his life.

Doctors said the child would die within weeks. Frightened for the life of their young son, his parents prayed earnestly for God's help; they prayed through enormous tears for healing.

After a few weeks had passed with the child receiving treatments the doctors discovered they could no longer see the tumor on the ultrasound. They tested the baby over and over again, but they could not understand what had happened – the tumor had simply disappeared!

Finally, the doctors could find no explanation and had to call it a miracle. That baby is now seven years old. God gave him extra time and no doubt has a plan for his life and for the lives of his parents. Praise the Lord!

Fighting Cancer

A very dear friend of mine was diagnosed with a rare form of cancer that affects various tissues and organs in the body, impairing their function.

The doctors had given little hope of recovery since the disease also affected her heart and liver and so at first they gave her just a few weeks to live.

Her faith prevailed though and after months of prayer, tears, chemo therapy and frustrating and gloomy predictions of outcome, my friend e-mailed me to say that the doctors believed she would only need one more chemo treatment. By the grace of God, the cancer cells would all be destroyed and she could return to a more normal life. We celebrated this miraculous news and rejoiced together.

As of this writing, however, cancer has appeared in yet another place in her body so it did not totally go away as the doctors had hoped. The miracle of this experience rests in something other than the outcome.

The miracle has come from the comfort of many praying friends, the strength received from her own children and blessed moments of hope. My friend has remained faithful, hopeful and strong throughout this experience and is a glowing testimony to others of God's love. That too, is a miracle.

The Miracle of the Sundial

Most of us take time for granted. Somewhere in the inter-section between faith and our busy lives, we've forgotten the admonition from Psalm 90 to

"number our days aright, that we may gain a heart of wisdom" (v. 12 NIV).

Yet, one of our most looming complaints concerns the lack of time available to accomplish all that we want to.

Hezekiah's Sundial

When God asked what He might do to prove to Hezekiah that He would indeed grant him the fifteen extra years of life, God gave him a choice that also involved a miracle of time.

God offered to move the clock, or the sundial in this case, ahead ten degrees or back ten degrees. The concept of degrees was identified more in terms of steps in that part of history, but the idea was that either of those choices would not be difficult for the Author of time.

Hezekiah, thinking that moving the clock ahead was a bit too easy for God, chose to have the Creator move the clock backwards instead. Scripture records that the shadow did indeed slip back ten steps as the sun once again took its place.

Since Hezekiah was too ill at the time to actually get out of bed, being able to look out on the sundial of Ahaz and see the shadow, was a great comfort to him.

He was given the gift of "believing is seeing."

What Is the Miracle?

Did the miracle occur when God answered Hezekiah's request to turn back the hands of time, or did the miracle occur when Hezekiah faithfully prayed that God would adjust the time of his life in spite of his illness?

My suggestion here is that perhaps the real miracle was that Hezekiah believed God would perform this deed, and so it was.

As people of faith, we need to examine our own perspective. Jesus often commented to His followers that if they only believed something would happen, it would.

"Therefore I tell you, whatever you ask for in prayer, believe that you have received it, and it will be yours" Jesus told us in Mark 11:24 NIV.

God Is Great!

What would it take for us to have more of the greatness of God? How can we wrap our faithful arms around the idea that God is very big and that He is the God of the possible? More than that, He is the God of the impossible.

As we live in a fast-paced, rushed world, where time gets away from us and runs out before we are ready, perhaps we can apply a little of Hezekiah's big faith to our own circumstances.

Perhaps we, too, can measure our days and experience the miracle of the full life God intended for us. Isn't it time?

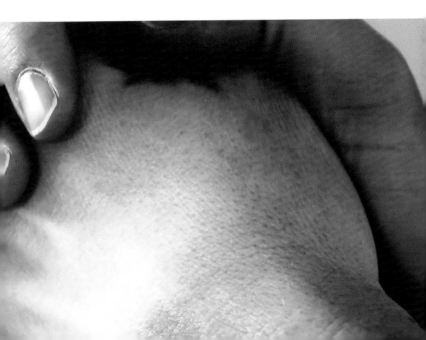

One More Quick Story

Several years ago another dear woman in my life was in the same position as Hezekiah. She found herself in the hospital, facing the possibility that her life would end.

As she was scheduled for surgery in the early morning, she went to sleep, or into a place where Jesus stopped by to say hello.

Standing beside her bed, Jesus told her that He had come for her and that it was time for them to go. Fearing the hardship that her death would mean for her husband, she asked the Lord for more time. She said she just believed it was important for her to stay a bit longer.

Jesus granted her request, but said that the next time He came, she would have to go. She agreed. Within moments, her fever lifted and her vital signs became stable.

The surgery was no longer necessary and the doctors were awed at her speedy recovery. Her faith had made her well.

Jesus granted her a Miracle Moment.

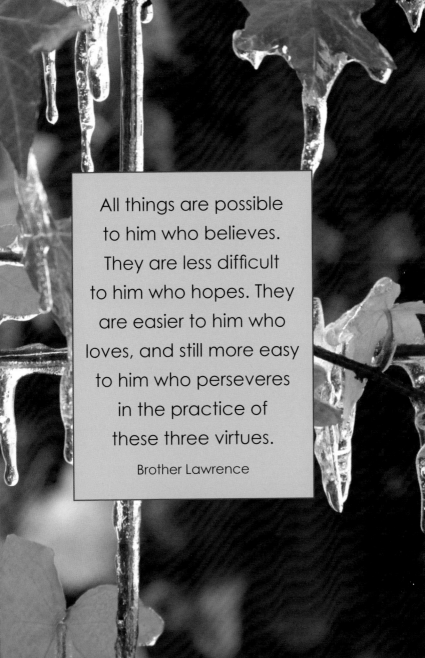

All things are possible
to him who believes.
They are less difficult
to him who hopes. They
are easier to him who
loves, and still more easy
to him who perseveres
in the practice of
these three virtues.

Brother Lawrence

Section Two
Miracle Moments of God's Provision

All that is good,
all that is true,
all that is beautiful,
all that is beneficent,
be it great or small,
be it perfect or fragmentary,
natural as well as
supernatural, moral as
well as material,
comes from God.

John Henry Newman

What in the World Is Happening?

The world is changing ... again. No matter where we live, we can see the impact of job loss, depleted resources, marginal health care and homelessness. We're bombarded with the news and it's rarely good.

We're overwhelmed by a sense that everything is out of control. So our challenge is to focus on the truth we know because of our faith in Christ. We must replace fear with faith, chaos with order, and natural with supernatural. We have only one Resource and He never changes. God is with us always, providing for our needs and watching out for our good.

Let's remind ourselves how His provision is made manifest by looking at some of the following biblical accounts.

God Feeds Elijah

If you remember Elijah's story you may recall that he was a prophet at the time that Ahab was ruling Israel with his something-less-than-sweet wife, Jezebel.

The marriage was a strong alliance for Ahab politically, but Jezebel's influence left a lot to be desired when it came to Israel's prophets.

No Rain, Ravens
and a Widow!

After Elijah proclaimed to Ahab that there wouldn't be any dew or rain on the land until Elijah said so, the Lord sent him off to a place to hide.

He set him beside a brook so he'd have water to drink and then he assigned some very special waiters to bring him food – ravens!

The Lord commanded the ravens to bring Elijah bread and meat every morning and every evening. We don't know if they were simply stealing these groceries from a nearby town, or if they were picking things up at God's general store, but they were providing what Elijah needed to stay alive.

This should be a reminder to us that God can use any of His creatures to serve Him. Eventually, the brook dried up and the food stopped coming, so Elijah knew it was time to move on.

And guess what? The Lord had already commanded a poor widow to feed him. What provision!

Flour Power

According to 1 Kings 17, Elijah was sent to a little town near Sidon where he met a woman gathering sticks. He asked her for some water and a little piece of bread.

The woman answered that she only had a little bit of flour and oil, and she was gathering sticks to make one last meal for herself and her son before they died of starvation.

Because the Lord had already prepared the way, however, the woman agreed to make a meal for Elijah. Elijah assured her that God had already promised her flour and the oil would not run out until the day God made it rain again to replenish the land.

The woman made the meal and she was able to make many meals for weeks afterward because the flour and the oil never ran out.

God provided.

God's Healing Power

A few weeks into this miraculous relationship, the woman's son became ill and he stopped breathing. The widow turned to Elijah for help, thinking that God had killed her son because of some past sins on her part.

Perhaps, like many of us, she never really understood God's power of forgiveness, or perhaps the presence of the man of God was just a strong reminder of her own past failings. Whatever it was, Elijah agreed to seek God's help in the matter.

Elijah took the widow's son to an upper room and, spreading his own body over the boy, he cried out to God three times to heal the boy and return his life to him. The Lord heard Elijah's cry and restored the boy to good health. The woman knew then that God indeed spoke through Elijah with words of truth.

Whether her son's illness was God's attempt to help her see His provision, since the never-ending flour and oil weren't really getting that message to her, is hard to know.

It's also possible that restoring her son to health was God reminding Elijah that He was indeed with him and providing for his needs.

Opening Our Own Eyes to God's Provision

As we look at God's provision in our own lives, what does it take for us to see and understand His clear presence? How do we recognize that He is continually watching out for our good in every circumstance?

One thing to consider is that when you answer God's call to do His work, He becomes your strength and your ally. He becomes your Resource for getting the job done. Your part is not always to create miracles, but to simply believe that He has entrusted you with a work to be fulfilled and that He will be with you always, guiding and providing for you in that work.

The prophets like Elijah accepted God's help and trusted it. We have that same option.

Let's look at another example of this and see what Elijah was able to do when Jezebel and the prophets of Baal sought to destroy the people's beliefs in the one true God.

Playing with Fire

When Elijah met up with Ahab, the king of Israel who was allowing people to worship the gods of Baal more than Yahweh, a pompous Ahab said this, "Is that you, you troubler of Israel?"

Isn't that an interesting question? Sometimes when you're doing the right thing, it's perceived as making trouble for the people who are enjoying their own decisions to do the wrong thing.

Ahab had nearly abandoned the God of Israel under Jezebel's influence and, though he may have lost sight of his own predicament, it was time for a showdown.

My God Against Your gods

In a somewhat Hollywood-movie style, Elijah proposed a little contest of "My God against your gods. Let's see who really has the fire!" Ahab accepted and they got on with the dueling.

At that point in time, Baal had 450 prophets and God had only Elijah because Jezebel had killed the rest of God's prophets. So Elijah tells Ahab to go first. He instructs him to build his altar, prepare some bulls, put the wood under the altar, but not to light the fire. The prophets could call out to their gods for that chore.

Well, those guys shouted till their throats were hoarse, and danced up a storm, but no fire rained down from the heavens. Elijah, enjoying the whole thing, taunted them a bit by suggesting that maybe their gods were traveling or in deep thought or maybe just too busy to answer their requests. Of course this made them shout all the more, but nothing happened.

Elijah's taunting just shows us how confident he was that God was with him and would show Himself in the situation. That kind of confidence is linked to Jesus' comment that we must pray believing if we expect to receive the answer.

Elijah's Turn

After several hours of all this frantic prophesying, Elijah finally called the people together to set up his own altar, his own bulls with some wood underneath them.

He even upped the ante a bit by drenching the bulls in water, digging a trench around them and filling it with water to make it even harder for a fire to start.

Finally, he called out to the God of the universe. He asked God to send a fire that would consume the bulls and turn the people's hearts back to Him.

One prophet, one request. No shouting, no frantic dancing; just one believing, faithful guy – and the fire rained down, burning up the sacrifice and consuming the bulls, the wood, the watered trench, and all that was around it. The people got the message.

They turned their hearts back to God and were on fire for Him again.

Becoming an Instrument of Belief

God provided all that was needed. Elijah was the instrument of belief that made it possible. You and I can be the instruments of belief for those around us. Our example, our hope, our fervent faith and our prayers help others believe too.

Whatever it is, we know for sure that God doesn't act without the faithful ones to help open the doors for Him. He never comes barging in without an invitation from one of His own.

Later, in another story, Elijah was fed twice by an angel so that he could travel for forty days and forty nights to the mountain of Horeb. That must have been some pretty powerful food to last him forty days.

> God provides in amazing ways to get the work done. He can provide what you need too.

Going into the Cave

When Elijah got to the cave where he was hiding, He called out to the Lord in his distress because he thought he was the only person left who was faithful to God.

It's interesting that after such an amazing miracle with Ahab and the gods of Baal that Elijah still felt alone when he got to the cave. Those times of total surrender and introspection can often make us feel alone, wondering if there are really any others who believe as we do.

It was a pleasant surprise to Elijah when God revealed He had preserved seven thousand others who were yet faithful to Him.

When You Feel Alone

It may be helpful to remember this story when you feel alone in your mission for God or wonder if anyone else believes as you do. When you answer God's call, He is always faithful to provide what you need.

He offers you food to nurture your body, friends to walk the way with you, and the means to get everything done.

You are never alone, for He is with you always. Sometimes, as you're hiding in the caves of darkness, having trouble sensing His light, you can't see that. As much as possible, seek the light again so that you can see God's provision in what may well be unexpected ways.

Where God Guides, He Provides

What do you need from God ... strength ... financial security ... love? Here are a few more quick examples of His provision to help fortify you today.

Sarah laughed at the idea of having a child in her advanced years, but God responded, "Is anything too hard for the LORD?" (Genesis 18:14 NCV). According to God's timing, Isaac was born.

When the people were mumbling as they left Egypt and followed Moses to the Promised Land, Moses answered them, "Stand firm and you will see the deliverance the LORD will bring you today" (Exodus 14:13 NIV).

A little further on in Exodus, we see that as Moses stretched his hands out over the sea, God drove the sea back with a strong east wind, creating dry ground for the children of Israel to pass through. When the Egyptians followed, they were all swept away as the waters returned. God provided the way for Israel.

God provided water for Moses and his followers with this instruction, "Speak to the rock before their eyes and it will pour out its water. You will bring water out of the rock for the community so they and their livestock can drink" (Numbers 20:8 NCV).

The greatest provision for any of us came through one means, God's beloved Son, which we're reminded of in John 3:16, "For God so loved the world that He gave His one and only Son that whoever believes in Him shall not perish but have eternal life" (NIV).

God Still Provides

A woman who was struggling during hard times to feed her family, a house full of growing boys, heard a knock on her front door. When she answered she met the face of a hungry man, emaciated, in great need of food.

Knowing she didn't have much in her own pantry, she told him to wait and she would get him whatever she could. She said as she started filling a bag for him with her meager supplies, that she had even more food.

She ended up giving the stranger four large bags of food and had more food left to feed her own family. Her willingness to give, even in her meager circumstances, gave God an open door and He provided a miracle.

A young man with a wife and two children had lost his job and was doing everything he could to continue to provide for them. One day a businessman stopped by his house to repossess his car, which was old and worn out, but still the only means of transportation the family had.

They hadn't been able to pay the loan on the car for several months and owed $300. Discovering that the family had little heat and no electricity, the businessman who had come for the car, changed his mind. He left and never said a word about taking the car. The next month, the young man learned that someone had paid off his bill.

God enriched the heart of a businessman and provided a miracle for a struggling family.

A single woman lost her job in her mid-fifties and the economy tightened up significantly, making it difficult to find a new job. She prayed for God's direction and for divine appointments at a trade show where she hoped to find some freelance opportunities. God provided the opportunity in the form of something she never expected.

She met a man who was also praying for help, and who lived in a city in Central America. She didn't speak Spanish. She'd never lived outside the United States. She walked in faith that this was God's plan and moved to a new country, safe in an environment that nurtured her faith, and provided for her in ways that she had never experienced before.

God provided enough income, but even more, a new quality of life. For her, it was a miracle.

A young man planted the seeds to start his own company. He built it on the foundation of spreading the seeds of God's love. He had only talent and faith in his tool box. He created a small line of bookmarks and watched it grow.

A few years later, he employed over thirty people and provided a way for more people to embrace their faith and renew their spirits. He planted, another watered, and God provided the increase. The company is still growing, blessed with unlimited faith in God's provision.

The stories are unending. The opportunities to receive God's provision are everywhere. See them in your friendships, in your abilities, and in your dreams made manifest. See them as receiving from the One who continues to watch over you, who watches out for you, and knows what you need even before you realize it yourself. See that receiving comes from believing.

As this reference from The Message says:
"The world is full of so-called prayer warriors who are prayer-ignorant. They're full of formulas and programs and advice, peddling techniques for getting what you want from God. Don't fall for that nonsense. This is your Father you are dealing with, and He knows better than you what you need. With a God like this loving you, you can pray very simply".

"Our Father in heaven,

Reveal who You are.

Set the world right;

Do what's best –

as above, so below.

Keep us alive with

three square meals.

Keep us forgiven with You

and forgiving others.

Keep us safe from

ourselves and the Devil.

You're in charge!

You can do anything You want!

You're ablaze in beauty!

Yes. Yes. Yes."

Matthew 6:7-13 (THE MESSAGE)

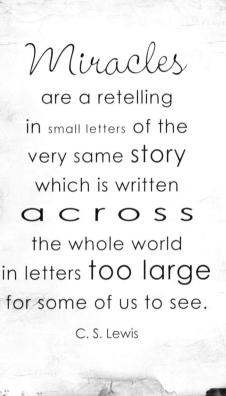

Miracles
are a retelling
in small letters of the
very same story
which is written
a c r o s s
the whole world
in letters too large
for some of us to see.

C. S. Lewis

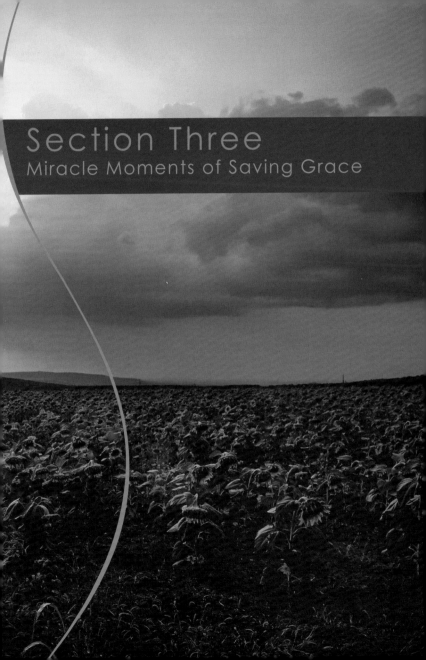

Section Three
Miracle Moments of Saving Grace

We believe
that the work of
regeneration,
conversion,
sanctification and
faith, is not an act
of man's free will
and power,
but of the mighty,
efficacious and
irresistible grace
of God.

Charles H. Spurgeon

The Miracle of Grace

As you wake up to a new day, you're completely covered. You don't have to think about it, beg for it, or figure out where to put it. In fact, you don't have to do anything at all because this one is totally a God thing.

God's gift to you and to me is His grace. It is grace we don't deserve and grace we miraculously received for only one reason:

God loves us.

Acts 20:32 shares a statement from Paul that says, "Now I commit you to God and to the word of His grace, which can build you up and give you an inheritance among all those who are sanctified" (NIV).

Again, in Ephesians 2:8-10, we are told, "For it is by grace you have been saved, through faith – and this not from yourselves, it is the gift of God – not by works, so that no one can boast. For we are God's workmanship, created in Christ Jesus to do good works, which God prepared in advance for us to do" (NIV).

These two verses and others like them help us to understand the very nature of grace and why it is indeed something of a miracle. This gift of grace is the one that sustains us through every action, every failure, and every success we experience.

Let's look at how grace played a significant part in the lives of some of our biblical family and how God continues to demonstrate that very sense of grace today.

The Beginning of the Grace of God

We may grasp the miracle of grace better if we examine the effort God made right from the beginning of human experience.

Our God of creation didn't miss a detail, and determining that it wasn't good for anyone to be alone, He created the animals in two's and created a partner for His servant, Adam.

When Adam and Eve slipped into temptation, God did not abandon them. He didn't allow them to live quite as innocently as they had before, but He didn't stop loving them.

He clothed them and fed them and watched over them.

When Noah's generation became so wicked in God's sight that He felt He needed to destroy them all and start over, He looked upon the events surrounding the flood and determined He would never take such an action again.

He made a promise to Noah's family to never flood His creation again. He covered the earth with grace and marked the Miracle Moment with a rainbow.

When God sent Abram out from the land of Haran to a new place, He gave Abram a new name and the opportunity to be a blessing to his descendants. When Abram lied to Pharaoh about his wife Sarai, saying that she was his sister, and Pharaoh took Sarai to be his wife, God intervened. He protected Sarai and let her return to her husband and her family. He extended grace to Sarai and Abram.

When Abraham and Sarah prayed continually for a baby, God's grace intervened. God answered them by making a new promise. He told Abraham that he would be the father of many nations and that his descendants would go on forever. A baby was born even in their old age.

From Isaac and Rebecca, Jacob and Rachel, Joseph and his brothers, the story continues of God's grace.

Each generation had people just like you and me who needed God to step in and offer another chance, another option, in spite of the wrongs they committed.

God's Grace to King David

Look at the grace God bestowed on a king who was in every way human, and yet yearned to be God's own man. David had a heart for God, but where would he have been without God's grace?

When David killed the giant, Goliath, God was with him. The young boy's spirit was fueled by his passion for the living God. He believed so completely that God was with him that nothing could stop him.

He ran into the battle and lifted his voice to the giant without fear or hesitation. He didn't need armor, he was covered from head to toe in an impenetrable grace, a force field the giant could never imagine.

Facing a giant takes big grace!

Being David Today

In modern-day circumstances, we each have to stand firm against the obstacles that threaten us, overwhelm us, and bully us into believing God no longer cares about us.

When you face obstacles, can you run toward them, so fully convinced that God is with you that you can take on anything?

Do you have His armor on so tightly that you have no fear whatsoever? What does it take for you to have the kind of faith and assurance that David had?

You might think it would take a miracle, but the truth is you already have the miracle. You have the saving grace of Christ and the opportunity every day to see His hand in all you do. You have the living Spirit of the One who called you ready to help you overcome every bully and every obstacle life may bring.

Sometimes the biggest obstacle to overcome is YOU.

You may have to gather a few stones of perception, experience, and persistence to help you slay the giants that hold you in fear.

You're Not Alone

You're not alone. Nearly everyone faces this battle one time or another. Any of us can fail to understand the truth of the abundant life God meant for us to have back in Eden or in our lives today.

We stand on fertile soil, but we don't always have the tools to break ground. Others that have gone before us paved the way, some saw the fruit of their labors and others made the path easier for us to walk. Here are a few examples from current history.

Thomas Edison was dyslexic, couldn't spell and was sent home from school because he was just "too stupid to learn anything." For a small boy, this kind of obstacle must have seemed powerful, even gigantic. It must have been a serious knock on the head for the school some years later when Edison became one of the greatest inventors of all time. Even educators need someone else to turn the light on sometimes.

When Arthur Blank and Bernard Marcus lost their jobs at a small home improvement center in the late 1970s, they joined forces with another friend, Ronald Brill, and started their own do-it-yourself warehouse. Today, Home Depot is one of the most successful franchises in the industry in America.

It always seems like we've been whacked by a giant and bullied into submission when we lose a job. We feel like we're left without any armor, and yet, sometimes, it's the biggest opportunity we will ever have. If we look for them, God has already prepared five smooth stones for each of us.

Fred Rogers's life changed the moment he saw a television set. With a heart for children, he began to look at the ways this powerful medium could be used to make children's lives happier and easier. He wanted to teach them some of the simple truths about life.

Mr. Rogers was an ordained Presbyterian minister who dedicated his life to guiding children to understand concepts like goodness and security. He took on the giant known as television and slew its misshapen and unguarded programs and offered new opportunities for viewers to see what it could mean to be a "good neighbor."

So How Else Do We Count Miracle Moments?

A Miracle Moment for you might have been the decision you made to marry your spouse, or to go to a particular college and study a degree that became a genuine calling. It might have been the time you were healed rather mysteriously of a broken toe or a tumor.

Maybe the biggest miracle was the one where you set your focus and your heart so much on God that you started to see His creativity in your life in a personal way.

What Triggers a Miracle Moment?

We saw that for King David, the shepherd boy, a Miracle Moment was his total belief in the living God to deliver him, to be with him, and to remove any obstacles.

For Thomas Edison, it was the belief that he had a purpose and that he couldn't fail in it. Even though it took him 2,000 tries to create the light bulb, he didn't see it as failing 2,000 times. He saw it as a 2,000-step process to get to success. Believing is seeing.

For Fred Rogers, it was television. Seeing a television triggered the opportunity for him to see how he could get his message across to millions of children and parents. It was a Miracle Moment and it was his faith that took him to the outcome.

Discovering Miracle Moments
for Yourself

Believe – Like David, you have to peel away any false sense of security, not weigh yourself down with the armor of the world. Go out in total confidence that the One who called you is faithful and ready to do everything from the mundane to the miraculous to make it possible for you to succeed. You have to go out with enthusiasm, as though the work you are doing is essential and no one can do it but you!

Be faithful – Like Edison, you might have to try more than once to get the result you're after, to get the miracle to happen. In fact, you may have to try 2,000 times before you arrive where you wanted to go. Every time your effort fails, every time the prayer seems to go unanswered, you have to get up, give God thanks for the new opportunity to try again, and get out of your own way to get things done. Every effort you make will be guiding you, teaching you, and helping you see the real miracle at work.

Be open – Like Fred Rogers, you have to be open to new ideas and directions. You have to look for possibilities to create miracles in places you may never have considered before. You have to capture the vision from a different angle and see it the way it most opens the way for God to come alongside you to make it happen.

You have to apply your gifts, your strengths, and the desires of your heart with every opportunity. You don't have to know how the miracle will happen, you just have to be open to the fact that God can indeed make it happen.

Be persistent – Like a child who learns to stand up again every time he falls, you have to be ready to fall, bounce back, and get on your way again. Miracles happen to people who believe in them, who know that God is always with them, always ready to bring about His purposes. Failing, at any level, in big ways and small ways, cannot deter the effort you are making to bring His purpose into being.

Like David, who fell and rose and fell again, you must persevere. Go back and read through Samuel if you need more reminders of the need for persistence in your desire to live a life that pleases your Creator.

Be ready – Perhaps most importantly, you have to be ready at any moment for your faith, your heart's desires, your purpose and vision to come together in a miraculous way. You have to be prepared to receive the very thing you're asking for.

Like the five maidens who kept the oil ready in their lamps while they waited for their bridegrooms, so you must be ready. Keep your oil burning, keep your vision in front of you, and when God's timing is perfectly aligned with His purpose for you, your miracle will happen.

You will be the conduit of His great plans.

The Hudson River Miracle

In January 2009, when US Airways flight 1549 landed in the Hudson River just moments after take-off, the passengers got wet, but they lived to talk about it.

Governor David Paterson said, "We had a miracle on 34th Street. I believe now we have had a miracle on the Hudson."

The pilot, Chesley Burnett Sullenberger III was credited with saving the lives of every passenger after what appeared to be a collision with a flock of birds. Somehow, with the grace of God, he managed to land the plane near midtown Manhattan in one of the busiest stretches of the Hudson River.

It Was a Plane Miracle!

For anybody who emerged safely from that plane, this incident was a miracle. Why this one was spared over others that ended tragically is only known to God.

The fact that it happened against great odds is a matter of record, but for those of us who choose to see God's hand at work in life at every possible intersection, it's a Miracle Moment of grace.

Getting More
Miracle Moments of Faith

The hope and purpose of a book like this is to remind you that miracles are not simply a fluke. Nor are they something that only happened to our biblical ancestors many years ago.

Perhaps we're struck by a sense that fails to recognize the miraculous because in our current world, we're bombarded with an influx of never-ending "realities." Things like reality TV shows keep us involved with more people's lives than a soap opera and cause us to stay so focused on "other" lives that we scarcely think about our own.

We don't have to get involved with wondering what else there is when we're not in touch with our own spirits, or our own sense of being.

Is it just "religious" people who experience miracles then? Can God create miracles for people other than those of us who profess to call upon Him? Not only can He, He does! In Isaiah 65:1 He says, "I made Myself known to people who were not looking for Me. I was found by those who were not asking me for help" (NCV).

God has sons and daughters all over the globe and He hears their cries and sees their needs for miraculous events. Sometimes He comes and makes His light shine in a way that blesses an individual or a whole community with His grace. Sometimes He uses people like you and me to help facilitate a miracle through our generosity, our prayers, or our gifts of intellect.

We were born miracles and life is a fascinating string of moments, interrupted by grace every time we allow it to be so.

How We Choose to See

Faith is a living,
busy, active, powerful thing;
it is impossible for it
not to do us good continually.

Martin Luther

Miracle Moments of faith are happening every day, all over the globe. In the past few weeks, God has given me a chance to witness His incredible and miraculous grace through "chance" meetings with people on airplanes, people that give me pause as I reflect on a conversation with them, or through gentle nudges of the Spirit as I go about my work.

The Butterfly

In my garden the other day, I noticed a beautiful yellow butterfly that got caught under the huge banana leaves that stand guard over the flowers like beach umbrellas.

The butterfly would rise up, get trapped under a leaf, then settle back down for a moment. It would rise again, only to be captured by yet more verdant soldiers.

Finally it found its way up and out and flew off into the blue sky, free to discover just where God would send it, fulfilling its purpose for being. For the butterfly, it was a Miracle Moment.

For me, as an observer, I realized how often the traps of life keep me from experiencing all God has for me.

I realized how important it is to keep rising, to keep persisting on the course set for me before I was even born.

Why Do We Need Miracle Moments?

We've been sent to earth to fulfill God's purpose and the Miracle Moments of faith are meant to give us wings to help us understand that we're a part of the whole, a part of all that God created for the good of this world.

We're God's miracles – serving, praying, lifting His Spirit into a world that is often stuck without realizing what has happened. Like the butterfly, we can even get trapped in the things that seem good, but still take away our freedom and never release our spirits.

I pray for you today, that Miracle Moments will lift you higher, filling your soul so much that you're not even sure your spirit can fit inside your body.

The truth is that when your spirit is aligned with the Spirit of the One who created you, it doesn't fit your body; it spills out everywhere you go, engaging, causing, celebrating with others who seek a miraculous faith. You're a walking miracle!

May you be blessed to discover the miracles that await you around the next corner!

At strategic
moments God
again and again
manifested Himself
to men by miracles
so they had
outward, confirming
evidence that the
words they heard
from God's servants
were true.

Billy Graham